Days Out From The Villages With Grandkids

Gillian Birch

Cover Photo: Gatorland - Orlando

ISBN-13: 978-1506108322

ISBN-10: 1506108326

**Dedicated to my wonderful grandchildren
Pippa, Jack, Daniel and Joseph**

Location Map

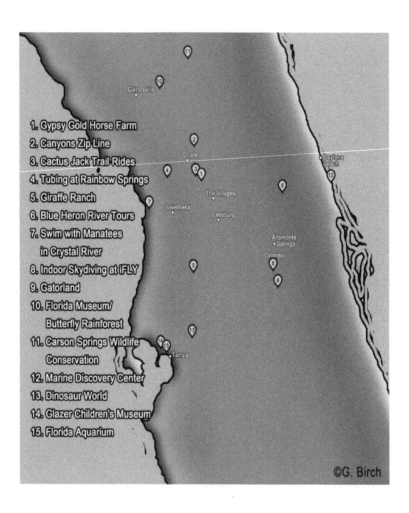

1. Gypsy Gold Horse Farm
2. Canyons Zip Line
3. Cactus Jack Trail Rides
4. Tubing at Rainbow Springs
5. Giraffe Ranch
6. Blue Heron River Tours
7. Swim with Manatees
   in Crystal River
8. Indoor Skydiving at iFLY
9. Gatorland
10. Florida Museum/
    Butterfly Rainforest
11. Carson Springs Wildlife
    Conservation
12. Marine Discovery Center
13. Dinosaur World
14. Glazer Children's Museum
15. Florida Aquarium

©G. Birch

CONTENTS

Preface

Having grandchildren to visit is always a special time. Most grandparents love to plan a highlight during the visit by doing something particularly special together. This book is full of great activities and adventures that can bridge the generation gap and be enjoyed by all ages from 2 to 92!

The best days out with grandchildren usually include animals, activities or adventures to create photo opportunities and happy memories that will be talked about for years to come. It's a delight to see youngsters' faces light up as they get up-close to tigers, swim with manatees, catch a sea star, ride a zip line or enjoy an activity that in their eyes is truly magical. With this book you can make it all happen, giving them some incredible experiences that they will never forget.

Animal Encounters

Animal lovers can enjoy a tour of a horse farm in Ocala or an African-style safari at the amazing Giraffe Ranch where you can handfeed giraffes, lemurs and other free-roaming exotic wildlife.

Tigers, lions, leopards and other exotic pets that have outgrown their use as cute props in commercial photographs all find a loving home at Carson Springs Wildlife Conservation. A visit to this spacious ranch offers the chance to interact with these beautiful creatures, see them at feeding time, and perhaps view newborn residents as part of the endangered animal breeding program.

More hands-on activities are outlined with chapters on Swimming with Manatees in the Crystal River, the only place in the world where this is possible. Alternatively, go horseback riding along the Cross Florida Greenway with a knowledgeable local guide.

If you want to introduce your grandkids to the "real" Florida, how about a visit to Gatorland, or take a trip on the St Johns River spotting all kinds of birds and wildlife on a Blue Heron River Cruise. The Marine Discovery Center also offers educational Discovery Cruises as visitors catch and identify a range of marine creatures such as horseshoe crabs, sea stars and conchs.

Educational Activities

Museums certainly don't have to be boring, as you will discover for yourself at the Florida Museum of Natural History and the Butterfly Rainforest in Gainesville. This fantastic research facility is one of the top attractions in the USA, providing an educational fun-filled day out for all ages, and it's free!

The Florida Aquarium is another excellent attraction and includes talks with divers actually inside the huge viewing tank. There are aquariums of sharks, giant rays, eels and barracuda as well as a 2-acre outdoor waterpark.

Younger children will love the hands-on play on offer at the Glazer Children's Museum where you can create your own weather and explore how locks work through water play. There are over 17 galleries where children can land an airplane, record a TV program, run a veterinary hospital or build a house using a crane. You'll be amazed at what this fantastic play area has to offer!

Action and Adrenaline!

If your teenage grandchildren want a little more action and excitement, we suggest some thrilling adrenaline-pumping activities at the Canyons Zip Line and Canopy Tours which is located in a beautiful forested canyon lakes landscape. Learn where to go tubing together near Rainbow Springs or consider a virtual skydiving experience in a safe but exhilarating wind tunnel.

Each chapter of *Days Out from The Villages with Grandkids* covers an attraction in full detail so you get a taste of what the attraction has to offer before you visit, enabling you to choose activities and attractions that best suit your family. The book also includes child-friendly places to eat out as part of your visit and it lists other nearby attractions if you want to extend your trip.

All these days out are less than 90 miles by car from The Villages and some are literally just up the road. Most of these attractions are surprisingly affordable. For example, you can swim with manatees for two hours including boat trip, wet suit and snorkel equipment for $45 – much cheaper than a day at Disney! Other attractions are completely free or only incur a nominal entrance fee or donation.

Whatever you choose to do when your grandchildren visit, I know you will have fun spending quality time together. Laugh and learn as you share these days out with your grandkids, building strong relationships and sharing precious moments. When you're done with these 15 exciting *Days Out from The Villages with Grandkids* there are 15 more ideas at the back of the book from my other Days Out from The Villages books. How's that for great value?

From one grandparent to another, I sincerely hope you enjoy planning and sharing these once-in-a-lifetime experiences with your grandchildren, creating unique memories that will last forever.

Happy Trails!

What's What

Introduction: Each destination begins with a short description of the attraction and what it offers, to help you choose a day out that will best suit your needs.

Location: Full address, contact details, website link and location make getting there very easy.

Directions: Distances are all calculated from the **CVS Pharmacy on 466** so directions and mileage should be adjusted from that point. It is at 5208 East County Road 466, The Villages, just in front of Publix Supermarket.

All destinations are less than 90 minutes' drive from The Villages and some are just down the road.

What to Expect: This section gives a full and detailed description of what the attraction has to offer, including guided tours, personal tips, best times to visit and other pertinent information for you to get the most from your visit.

Where to Eat: These are all family-friendly places that I have personally experienced and would happily go back to. The businesses did not know I was gathering information for a book; I was simply there as an ordinary paying customer.

Cost: Admission prices and cost of boat trips, guided tours etc. are all correct at time of going to press in early 2015. They are intended as a guideline only and may be subject to change in the future.

Opening Times: I have supplied general information, telephone numbers and website links. It is advisable to call and confirm details before setting off, to avoid disappointment.

Nearby Attractions: Once you have enjoyed visiting your chosen destination, other nearby attractions are suggested to extend your day out or include as a detour on your journey home.

Gypsy Gold Horse Farm Tours

You may be surprised to learn that the most popular visitor attraction in Ocala is the Gypsy Gold Farm Tour. This attraction focuses on the graceful Gypsy Vanner Horses that were bred specifically to pull gypsy caravans in Europe, long before the motorvan was invented. The tours are full of interest for all ages, particularly those with an interest in horses and gypsy history.

This unforgettable tour introduces you to the beautiful Gypsy Vanner Horses with their "feathered" feet, long silky manes and colorful markings. You will also meet the man responsible for introducing the breed to the USA and learn a little about the story behind his passion for Vanner horses.

One particularly interesting fact I learned during my visit was that gypsies live in extended family groups. Often the grandchildren were responsible for caring for the horses, moving the stakes daily so the horses could enjoy fresh grazing. These horses have been part of the extended gypsy family for generations, making a visit with your grandchildren a particularly poignant day out.

Location
Located off 475A just north of Hwy 484.

Gypsy Gold Horse Farm
12501 SW 8th Ave
Ocala
FL34473
Tel: (352) 817-3777 or 1-866-497-7982

www.gypsygold.com

What to Expect on a Visit to Gypsy Gold Horse Farm
Ocala is surrounded by horse farms, equestrian training and stud facilities so it's really exciting to get the opportunity to see what's beyond the gates at the Gypsy Gold Horse Farm. The farm is owned and run by Dennis Thompson who, along with his late wife Cindy, introduced the Gypsy Vanner Horse breed to the USA in 1996.

Their passion for the breed began on a visit to a gypsy horse fair in Appleby, England. A strange encounter with a fortuneteller began the couple's destiny with gypsies and their Vanner Horses.

The Thompsons imported the first 16 Gypsy Vanner Horses to North America and founded the Gypsy Vanner Horse Society in 1998. Dennis tells an amazing and emotional story which you and your grandchildren will no doubt remember long after the visit is over.

Dennis has a deep passion and respect for these graceful horses which you will see running free in the surrounding paddocks. The breed comes in many different colors including piebald (black and white), skewbald (brown and white) and solid colors, as you will learn from the short informative talk at the start of the tour.

Dennis is also a fount of knowledge about the gypsy culture as these horses were selectively bred to pull the round-topped caravans that the European gypsies called home. Gypsy Vanner Horses are like small Shire Horses with their distinctive feathers (hair below the knees) and large hooves. Their flowing manes and tails are luxuriant and silky, making these beautiful horses look like they are flying when they canter at speed around the pastures!

However, the selective breeding was more about the horses' sweet disposition, intelligence and docility rather than their looks. These horses had to be trusted with pulling the loaded vans, hence the name "vanner", and yet be gentle and tolerant with the younger members of the extended gypsy family.

The tour moves around the farm as visitors are introduced to many of the horses, foals and other animals that live there. The kids will love feeding treats to the horses such as cut up carrots and apples. Dennis provides these as part of the tour, but you're welcome to bring your own contributions to donate to the "treat fund."

At the end of your visit, you and your grandkids will no doubt have fallen in love with this beautiful horse breed and will depart with a new respect for true gypsies and their nomadic way of life.

Additional Information
Reservations are required for all tours which last for around 2 hours. Once you have purchased your tickets online you can select the day you want to attend, space permitting.

Tours book up fast so you need to plan ahead, particularly in school holidays.

Admission
Tickets $30 per person on arrival; $25 per person if pre-purchased online.

Discounts for seniors and children under 5.

Private tours behind the scenes are also available for 2-4 persons at $100.

Opening Times
Tours are offered on Wednesdays and Saturdays at 10 a.m.

Private tours for groups and families can be reserved at other times by prior arrangements.

Where to Eat near Gypsy Gold Horse Farm
You might want to round off your horse-themed day out with a meal at the lovely Horse and Hounds Pub on E. Silver Springs Blvd. (US-40) in Ocala. This English-style pub has a great menu including some British favorites such as Shepherd's Pie, Guinness Beef Stew and Fish and Chips (with mushy pies on the side!). This restaurant provides an appropriate end to your visit to Gypsy Gold with a relaxed casual atmosphere and a great range of beers.

Nearby Attractions
- Silver River State Park
- Marjorie Kinnan Rawlings Historic State Park
- Cactus Jack Trail Rides
- Don Garlits Museum of Drag Racing

Canyons Zip Line and Canopy Tours

Who'd have thought you could find 70-foot cliffs, limestone canyons and hills that are just perfect for zip lining in the heart of Central Florida? That was the challenge for Traci and Bobby Walker when they scoured the length and breadth of Florida looking for the perfect naturalized environment for their zip lining adventures and thrilling canopy tours.

They found exactly what they were looking for just 34 miles from The Villages in 100 acres of hilly forested terrain which was used for mining until the 1920s. What man and nature created between them is an awesome landscape of hills and valleys. The sheer chalk cliffs, caves, ridges and lakes are just begging to be zipped over, rappelled down and traversed across using rope bridges in a very eco-friendly manner. If the spectacular natural scenery doesn't take your breath away, the zip lines certainly will!

Location
Located on Hwy 25A just one mile east of I-75 Exit 358.

Canyons Zip Line and Canopy Tours
8045 NW Gainesville Rd
Ocala
FL34475
Tel: (352) 352-9477

www.zipthecanyons.com/

What to Expect on a Visit to the Canyons Zip Line
If you're looking for some adrenalin-pumping activity in a beautiful natural area then Canyons Zip Line and Canopy Tours are just the thing for you. Accompanied by two professionally certified guides, full tours take in 9 zip lines, 2 swaying rope bridges, 5 lakes and a rappel descent as part of an unforgettable 2 ½ hour experience just outside Ocala.

Nervous beginners and zip line virgins may prefer to start with a shorter Canyons Tour which offers 90 minutes of soaring, climbing, zipping and flying.

If you want to see the stunning scenery and natural landscape at a quieter pace, the Canyons also offer guided horseback rides through the 100-acre private property which remains largely undisturbed. The eco-friendly owners employ an arborist to take care of the many trees, including a 300-year-old landmark live oak with contorted spreading branches and a 400-year-old cedar.

Zip lining is suitable for anyone over the age of 10, but you must be between 70lbs and 270lbs to ensure that you are heavy enough to ride the zip lines at a safe speed using the gravity-fed system. Older age is certainly no barrier as two local ladies, aged 96 and 93 respectively, both completed the full zip lining course recently and are apparently ready to do it all again!

Your zip lining experience starts with a ride in the onsite bus or ATV to the Ground School location. Here your instructors will teach you the rudiments of flying through the air. You are securely clipped into a hang-gliding harness at all times using a two-lanyard safety system. Once everyone has mastered the training zip line and feels comfortable to start, the tour moves on to the real thrills. Initial flights start about 17 feet above terra firma with short bunny zips transporting you through the trees from one elevated landing stage to the next.

The zip lines get progressively higher and longer as your confidence grows until you are ready to take on the longest, highest and fastest zip lines in Florida. The final flight is followed by a rappel to the ground to end your thrilling canopy tour.

The exhilarating tour includes zip lines of around 600 feet in length transporting you across flooded quarries formed by man and gently weathered by nature to create a surreal adventure in the tree tops. Flights start from tree stands or from the edge of sheer limestone cliffs where you launch yourself off and the ground suddenly drops away leaving you travelling at speed across lakes and greenery far below.

Some zips have earned special names such as "No return" where the tower has no steps. If you zip in, the only exit is to zip out again. Another favorite point is "Walk the Plank" which is probably the only place in Florida where you can literally jump off a cliff! A professional photographer is employed to capture some of your daring flights to ensure you have a great memento of your awesome Canyons zip lining adventure.

Safety is paramount, as owner Traci puts it: "Riders do the zipping and we do the clipping" to ensure complete safety. All zip lines are secured to solid concrete pads and have an overhead safety cable. Even the smallest tours have two guides – one at the front and one at the rear. With tours departing every 20 minutes, the 40 staff are certainly kept busy.

The Canyons Zip Line has been open since 2009 and the enterprising owners of this family-run business have plans to expand. Currently they can accommodate corporate groups of visitors from 200-600, but singles, couples and families are equally welcome to sign up for a treetop adventure together.

Future plans include overnight camping on the clifftops, taking advantage of the superb bass fishing in the lakes, and possibly even caving in some of the newly discovered caves in the hillside.

One thing is for sure, this is one business that is definitely not standing still!

Additional Info

The Canyons also offers horseback riding around this peaceful traffic-free estate. Horseback riders are taken from the Welcome Center to the stables in ATVs where their mounts will be saddled and ready to go.

The 100-acre property has many pleasant pastures for the horses to graze and plenty of natural woodland scenery for riders to enjoy. The 90-minute horseback rides take in plenty of sandy trails with uphill and downhill descents, skirting lakes and offering superb viewpoints from the clifftops.

Admission

90 minute Canyons Express (5 zip lines and one rope bridge) $59.00 per person

2½ hour Full Zip/Canopy Tour (9 zip lines, 2 rope bridges and a rappel) $96.00 per person

Super Zip $30.00 (side by side double racing zip which is hands free!)

90 minute Horseback Tours $60.00 per person

Opening Times
Open daily 9 a.m. to 5 p.m.

Where to Eat near Canyons Zip Line
Canyons Gift Shop sells snacks and drinks, otherwise make a detour into Ocala for food.

There are a couple of good family-friendly restaurants near the Paddock Mall. Gators Dockside on SW 42nd St has a family fun night on Tuesdays from 5-8pm. There's a magician and kids under 12 eat free!

Another popular choice with older grandkids is the Melting Pot in Ocala where you can share a leisurely meal cooking meat, seafood and vegetables in a hot cheese fondue followed by dipping fruit and cookies in a chocolate fondue. They'll love it!

Nearby Attractions
- Rainbow Springs State Park
- Gypsy Gold Horse Farm
- Cactus Jack Trail Rides

Cactus Jack Trail Rides

Located just north of The Villages at the entrance to the Land Bridge Trail Head, Cactus Jack Trail Rides offers a relaxing way to enjoy Florida's green open spaces, oak hammocks and pine forests. These relaxed trail rides on horseback show off the beauty of nature in the Ocala area, which is, after all, the Horse Capital of the World!

The trail rides are all on traffic-free routes. They use public trails within the Cross Florida Greenway State Park which actually connects the Gulf of Mexico with the St Johns River. This 110-mile greenway corridor of land was designated for the historic Florida Ship Canal project which was never completed. It is now a valuable recreational resource for biking, horseback riding, hiking and other outdoor activities. As it is right on the doorstep of The

Villages, it's a great area to bring the grandkids and enjoy a horseback riding experience together.

Location
Located at the entrance to the Land Bridge Trail Head on South Hwy 475A.

Cactus Jack Trail Rides
11100 SW 16th Ave
Ocala
FL34480
Tel: (352) 266-9326

www.cactusjackstrailrides.com

What to Expect on a Cactus Jack Trail Ride
Cactus Jack horses are stabled offsite overnight and are transported to the Land Bridge Trail Head location each morning in horseboxes. You'll see the sign on the gate as you drive into the car park. The horses stand in shady open stalls ready to be saddled up and ridden out along some of Florida's most scenic trails within the Cross Florida Greenway State Park.

Riders should arrive at the entrance to the Land Bridge Trail Head about 30 minutes before your prebooked time. This allows plenty of time to sign paperwork, don a helmet (optional) and get mounted. Don't worry, there's a useful mounting block to help riders get safely and easily into the saddle of even the largest horses!

What's so great about this particular trail ride is that it is completely traffic free with underpasses beneath the 475 and 475A highways. The rides are led by local guides with many years riding experience.

Cactus Jack has many different horse breeds including Quarter Horses, Paints, Thoroughbreds, Rocky Mountain Horses, Argentine Polo Ponies and even a Percheron. They are sourced from all over the USA as former ranch ponies, polo ponies, rescue horses and even one horse that has Mounted Police Training. What they all have in common is a gentle nature. They are all well fed, fit, healthy and are clearly well loved by owner Deb, husband Jamie, and their experienced team of guides.

Cactus Jack Trail Rides cater for all levels of riding ability, from novice upwards, so let them know what riding experience you have. They carefully match horses with riders according to size, weight and levels of experience so everyone gets a safe and enjoyable ride. Unfortunately they are only insured to take riders aged 6 and up.

You can book rides of various lengths but usually one or two hours is long enough for non-riders and seniors to be nicely stiff the following day! Custom rides are also available – just phone up and make your request.

Cactus Jack Rides take a variety of different routes through the Greenway depending upon the season and the temperature. The two-hour rides generally head west, crossing the busy I-75 on the Land Bridge following a figure 8 route out and back. Shorter rides usually head northeast along the Florida Trail and all the routes are exceptionally scenic and pretty. Most of the rides are in shady areas so you can enjoy riding at a relaxed pace through pine forests, oak hammocks and open meadows. It is so peaceful with just the sound of birds and insects; the rest of the world seems very far away!

Some of the wildlife that previous riders have seen include a Great Horned Owl, rare Fox Squirrels, soaring Red-tailed Hawks, Pileated Woodpeckers with their scarlet cap, Virginia Quail, Red-Shouldered Hawks, Sandhill Cranes, Red Cardinals, Foxes, Gopher Tortoises, Armadillos, Corn Snakes, Black Racers and even a Coyote!

Those with previous riding experience will get the chance to trot and canter at suitable points during the ride, but beginners can maintain the pace they are happy at. What Cactus Jack Trail Rides are all about is enjoying the ride in stunning scenery and sharing the wonderful experience with family and friends.

Additional Information
Riders should wear long pants and closed-toe shoes for comfort and safety. If it's sunny you should wear sunscreen or cover your arms with a long-sleeve shirt.

Admission
$45 per person for a one hour accompanied trail ride

$55 per person for a 90 minute ride

$65 per person for a two hour ride

Opening Times
Cactus Jack Trail Rides are available daily by prior reservation.

Rides are generally scheduled for 9 a.m., 1 p.m. and 3.30 p.m. but times can be adjusted on request.

Where to Eat near Cactus Jack's

After your ride you may want to visit the Cracker Barrel Old Country Store for a meal which is just two miles down the road.

Alternatively, bring a picnic or drinks and make use of the picnic tables at the Land Bridge Trail Head State Park.

If you fancy stopping for ice cream on the way home, try Brusters on Mulberry Plaza (Hwy 42) as you return to The Villages via Buena Vista Blvd, or head for Baskin Robbins near Publix on Wedgewood Lane (Hwy 466).

Nearby Attractions
- Gypsy Gold Horse Farm
- Don Garlits Museum of Drag Racing
- Rainbow Springs State Park

Tubing at Rainbow Springs State Park

Rainbow Springs State Park has many great outdoor activities for families at any time of year. The clear spring waters provide endless entertainment for visitors looking for fun on the Rainbow River. It's a great place to enjoy swimming, snorkeling, kayaking and canoeing in the beautiful clear waters of Florida's fourth largest spring, and it's much closer than going to the beach!

One of my favorite activities has to be tubing gently down the Rainbow River - a beautiful way to spend a hot summer's day with the grandkids. However, you have to get there early on weekends as the tubing area quickly reaches full capacity and the gates are closed.

The tubing area is open from the first Saturday in April through the end of September. It is fantastic fun for all ages, especially when it's too hot to do anything else!

Location
Located 3 miles north of Dunnellon on Hwy 41

Rainbow Springs State Park
19158 SW 81st Place Road
Dunnellon
FL34432
Tel: (352) 465-8555

NB. There is a separate entrance for tubing on SW 180th Avenue Road, Dunnellon.

http://www.floridastateparks.org/rainbowsprings/

What to Expect on a Visit to Rainbow Springs State Park

Rainbow Springs is an extensive state park which was once a private wildlife attraction. All that remains of that early enterprise are the renovated cultural gardens which have stunning azalea blooms in early spring. There is also a native plants garden which attracts many butterflies and hummingbirds in summer.

Rainbow Springs State Park was created around the headsprings of the Rainbow River which bubbles out from several vents producing around 600 million gallons of fresh water per day. It quickly becomes a broad river of clear warm water which flows past K.P. Hole, where there is limited tubing, and past Blue Cove towards Dunnellon.

The park includes areas of mixed forest, sandhills, wetlands and flatwoods and you may spot squirrels, hawks, owls, whitetail deer, river otters, wading birds, turtles, gators and fish including bass. The park has a 2½ mile nature trail with overlooks of the river and the phosphate pit that was once mined here.

If you enjoy bird watching, you will find many opportunities for birding along the trails or from the river. The park also offers guided bird walks with a ranger on the second Saturday of the month from September through May.

By far the most popular activities at Rainbow Springs State Park are swimming and snorkeling in the designated area of the river. Canoes and kayaks are available for hire and are a fun activity for children who are able to swim. It is one of the best ways to enjoy the river, its wildlife and the surrounding scenery.

Tubing Down the Rainbow River
One thing that makes Rainbow Springs unique is the wonderful tubing it offers. It's an amazing sight to see the river bobbing with a flotilla of colorful bathing-suited visitors all drifting downstream in an ongoing parade.

Floating gently downstream on a rubber tube is such a relaxing way to enjoy the passing scenery. You can try holding hands or even tie tubes together as you journey downriver. Coolers, alcoholic drinks and disposable containers are prohibited on the river by local ordinance so leave drinks and snacks in the car for enjoying later. The trip takes around two hours and the grandkids will probably want to hop back on the tram and do it all over again!

The best place to launch your tube is at the dedicated tubing area located on the back road to the state park, about 8 miles downstream from the headspring. Access is from SW 180th Avenue Road off Hwy 484 east of Dunnellon.

The original tubing launch area was at the K.P. Hole County Park where there is still limited tubing on the west side of the river. This is a longer float covering the upper and lower river ending at the SR 484 bridge in Dunnellon. It takes about four hours to complete. Huge demand, limited car parking and overcrowding at K.P. Hole led to the development of the new tubing area on the east side of the state park. It has its own separate access point, restrooms and other facilities. Park admission is payable at the entrance to the car park.

The concessionaire transports you by shuttle from the car park about two miles upstream to the tubing launch point. You gradually drift back down the river, beneath moss-draped cypress trees in crystal clear waters that are often over five feet deep. The trip takes up to two hours, depending upon the wind and water conditions.

Once your tubing is over you can drive around to the main headsprings entrance to the park to continue enjoying swimming, picnicking and walking in the gardens as part of your paid admission – just show your receipt at the entrance.

Additional Information
The tubing facilities can reach maximum capacity on weekends so it's worth going early or calling the park (352-465-8525) to check availability before leaving home.

Admission
Admission to the state park is $2 per person; $5 per vehicle.

Tubing fee $11 per person. This includes tubing equipment and tram shuttle to the tubing launch area.

Opening Times
Rainbow Springs SP is open daily 8 a.m. to sundown.

The Tubing Entrance is open April through September from 8 a.m. to 5 p.m. Last access for tubing is 3.30 p.m.

Where to Eat at Rainbow Springs State Park
There are picnic pavilions, tables and grills overlooking the main spring basin so bringing your own food and drink is the best way to enjoy a meal as part of your visit.

Dunnellon has many local restaurants including the Pizza Joint on W. Dunnellon Road which has the only wood burning pizza oven in Citrus County!

I often stop in at the Blue Gator Tiki Bar and Restaurant on Hwy 41 in Dunnellon when I am passing through. It has a delightful beer garden overlooking the Withlacoochee River and is a friendly place to stop for drinks or a meal.

Nearby Attractions
- Crystal River Venture (Swimming with Manatees)
- Cooter Pond Park, Inverness

Giraffe Ranch

Wherever your grandkids are visiting from, unless they live in Africa they are unlikely to have giraffes in their backyard. Here at The Villages, we have the amazing Giraffe Ranch within easy driving distance, located between Brooksville and Dade City on Hwy 301.

This exotic animal encounter offers wildlife safaris in open-sided 4x4 vehicles, by Segway or even riding high on camels in the ultimate eco-adventure.

Expect to see and interact with ostriches, antelopes, zebras and giraffes in a natural open environment. It's just like an African safari without the airfare. How's that for something truly special!

Location
Located about 35 miles south of The Villages just off Hwy 301 between Brooksville and Dade City.

Giraffe Ranch
38650 Mickler Rd
Dade City
FL33523
Tel: (813) 482-3400

www.girafferanch.com/

What to Expect on a Visit to Giraffe Ranch
Giraffe Ranch is a family owned and operated game park and wildlife preserve on 47 acres of rolling grassland adjoining the Green Swamp Wilderness Area. It is home to an amazing collection of exotic wildlife as well as other wild Florida animals and birds that drop in, such as threatened sandhill cranes.

Drive in through the gates of the ranch and appreciate the quiet open space with huge live oaks, lush pastures and natural wetlands that suit the many different species of animals from Africa, Asia, Australia and the Americas. Run by Lex Salisbury (former director of Lowry Park Zoo) and his wife Elena, Giraffe Ranch is much more natural than a zoo as there are no cages and pens. Tours are limited to 20 people per truck and must be booked in advance, making it a very uncrowded and enjoyable experience. Tours take place twice a day at 11am and 2pm.

Each tour starts with an informative chat from the owner/guide and then there's the chance to visit the petting area before getting onboard the trucks for your safari expedition. You ride in customized safari vehicles just like an African safari. The elevated bench seats and open sides give everyone a good view and the chance to take some great photographs as animals approach. The vehicles have shady canopies and you'll find the breeze keeps you cool as your safari guide drives you around the various habitats.

Part of the tour is a stop to hand feed the giraffes, which is absolutely thrilling! They know trucks mean food and they come right up and stick their long necks into the truck. Who doesn't want to feed a giraffe and smell its grassy breath as it leans down to take eat leaves right from your hand with its 18 inch long black tongue?

These exciting tours last about 90 minutes, and will quickly have everyone excitedly spotting animals. It's a unique opportunity to get up-close to free-roaming animals including giraffes, hippos and rhinos. You will also see specialist herds of miniature Dexter cattle from Ireland and Haflinger horses from Austria. It's a real joy to see different species living peaceably together and interacting quite naturally with each other. There are herds and families of zebras, ostriches, goats, giraffes and other animals with their young in tow, particularly in the summer months.

If you want something even more different, consider a camel safari. Apparently the camels love it and line up at the gates each morning to go to "work." You will be helped to mount these kneeling humpbacked beasts. They lurch and sway as they stand and then easily carry you around the reserve to view the herds of game animals. Another high-tech option is a safari on a Segway which puts you at ground level as you meet the residents of Giraffe Ranch.

Other animals at Giraffe Ranch include stripy zebras, cute baby giraffes, rare breeds of giant tortoises, an ugly warthog called Fred, a zedonk (you'll find out the story on your safari), fluffy ostrich chicks, bongos (antelopes), a spiny African crested porcupine, lethal-looking scimitar horned oryx and various camels, blackbucks and other mammals. All the animals look healthy, happy and very well cared for as well as being free to roam as they please. The guides are always on hand to assist and answer any questions as part of your memorable visit.

After enjoying your safari with a knowledgeable ranger/guide you get the chance to interact with some of the animals which is thrilling for children of all ages. You can pet camels, stroke their soft nose and see their broad hooves and long lashed eyes which make them perfect "ships of the desert."

Other add-on experiences include a short camel ride, otter feeding, behind the scenes tours, and feeding the hippos and hosing them down, which they love! You can also interact with the cute ring-tailed lemurs who love to be handfed grapes.

Part of the visit includes the petting enclosure with tortoises, monkeys, guinea pigs and other animals. Finally, there's a gift shop with animal-themed souvenirs, drinks and snacks.

Although this day out is certainly not cheap, it is truly wonderful to see grandchildren's faces light up as they feed and interact with these amazing exotic animals. Compared to a zoo, it is so much more rewarding, and compared to Disney's Animal Kingdom it's a bargain day out!

Additional Information
Discount coupons are sometimes available on Groupon so it's worth checking out.

Admission
Buggy Safari $75 per person for all ages. Discount for groups.

Camel Safari $150 (must be over 3 years of age).

Segway Safari $150 (must be over 14 years of age and weigh between 100 and 300 lbs).

Opening Times

Open daily. Tours depart at 11 a.m. and 2 p.m. and places must be prebooked.

Where to Eat near Giraffe Ranch

If you want lunch either before or after your visit to Giraffe Ranch you should head south to Dade City. There's a KFC right on US 301, Pizza Hut on the North 98 Bypass and Beef O'Bradys on 7th Street if you're looking for burgers and wings.

Nearby Attractions

- Pioneer Florida Museum and Village
- Dinosaur World
- Florida Aquarium
- Glazer Children's Museum

Blue Heron River Tours

The chance to enjoy a peaceful couple of hours wildlife spotting on the St Johns River has to be a winner when it comes to bridging the generation gap. This tour is on a large and spacious pontoon boat (seats 50+) which has a toilet and a small refreshments area onboard – both essential for happy grandkids in my experience!

The scenic eco-friendly trip has so much wildlife you'll be spotting birds, manatees, alligators and nests before you've even left the marina! In my opinion it's well worth the slighter longer journey to DeLand for this boat trip as it has much more to see than other boat tours closer to The Villages.

Location

Located off US-44 west of DeLand at Hontoon Landing Resort on Lake Beresford

Blue Heron River Tours
Hontoon Landing Resort and Marina
2317 River Ridge Road
DeLand
FL34236

Tel: (386) 873-4843

NB. Check the address on Google maps before leaving as the actual marina is not easy to find. Once you turn off Hwy 44 the journey is slow, so allow plenty of time or the boat may sail without you!

http://blueheronrivertours.com

What to Expect on a Blue Heron River Tour

This two-hour eco/nature tour is crammed with action and wildlife sightings from the moment you step aboard the very comfortable boat. Every seat has a good view, but there's plenty of opportunity to move around, take photographs and see plenty of wildlife as you explore the "real" Florida.

Check in at the resort reception then browse the well-stocked store. You don't need to bring any drinks or snacks as the boat has a selection of snacks for sale in the rear galley area for $1, payable on an honor box system. You can also hire binoculars onboard if you have forgotten to

29

bring any – very useful for seeing the birds, flowers and deer in detail during the trip.

From the dock you will see boats of all sizes moored in this peaceful marina right on the banks of the dark swirling waters of the St Johns River. This broad waterway was once busy with paddlewheelers transporting passengers, timber and other goods up and down the waterway between Jacksonville, Sanford and the lake system beyond. Now it is quietly enjoyed by pleasure boaters, fishing enthusiasts and ecotourists.

The St Johns River is the only river in the USA that flows from south to north. From its headwaters near Melbourne, the river flows at a gentle pace of less than 1 mph for over 300 miles until it reaches the Atlantic Ocean near Jacksonville.

During your trip you will see why the Seminoles called this the "River of Lakes" as it widens out into huge lake-like areas during its lengthy journey. The trip visits one of these, Lake Beresford, along with the St Johns River, Hontoon Dead River and one of several canals created in the 1800s by the army to make the journey straighter and deeper for the unwieldy paddlewheelers.

Wildlife on the St Johns River
Your friendly captain will introduce himself and give you some idea of what you might see during your natural Florida adventure, but every trip is different. In summer the gators tend to be submerged to keep cool and the migratory birds are gone, but to compensate the banks are blooming

with amazing plants, trees and epiphytes. Learning about the history of the St Johns River, the Indian totem poles that have been discovered, seeing huge alligator nests and the indigenous wildlife such as herons, anhingas, eagles, deer, raccoons and bears provides plenty of interest.

Winter tours on the river provide many sightings of alligators basking in the wintry sunshine, manatees feeding and swimming along the river, and of course many migratory bird species.

As you leave the marina you will see many multi-million dollar properties and boat docks that have replaced the 1950s fish camps that once lined the banks of Hontoon Island. Incidentally, part of the island is now a state park which is free to visit, accessed by a ferry service run by the park rangers.

The quiet calm of the river soon starts to weave its spell as you listen to the sounds of birds, wildlife and water gently lapping the boat as it progresses along. The tour is described as being an "interactive eco tour" and everyone is expected to point out possible sightings of wading birds, nesting ospreys, soaring eagles, gators and flowering plants.

Smooth "footprints" on the river surface usually denote the presence of a manatee surfacing to breathe and feed. As the boat slows to investigate you may see the telltale nose appear, followed by the large fan tail as these gentle giants enjoy a somewhat treacherous existence in conflict with boat propellers, fishing lines and other manmade hazards.

During my December trip we saw families of coots running along the water's surface, a red shouldered hawk perched ready to hunt, anhingas spreading their wings to dry, many white ibis with their bubblegum-pink legs and curved beaks, egrets, a beautiful osprey eating a fish on a high branch, several rare limpkins hunting for apple snails, black vultures, a bald eagle, blue herons, little blue herons (including some white juveniles) and the prettiest gallinules strutting over the pennywort. We were also fortunate enough to see a pied-billed grebe which our guide identified for us.

Captain Bob gave us plenty of facts and information about each different species we saw. He kept up a running commentary on the different types of trees, flowering epiphytes, balls of mistletoe and other endangered vegetation, along with some light humor. There was certainly never a dull moment!

When we reached the entrance to the Blue Springs State Park we saw many manatees including a Mom and baby swimming in the crystal clear headwaters of the springs. They love to hang out here during cold snaps as the spring waters bubble up at a steady 72F to provide the warm water these mammals need to survive. Everyone on the boat was spellbound and we were happy to linger and watch these huge sea cows feeding, diving and surfacing from time to time.

One of the highlights of the boat trip was sailing through an old cut which was dug by hand in the 1800s. The narrow waterway provided the chance to see deer, possum and turkeys in the dense greenery on either side. This is an opportunity to experience Florida in the raw, with its variety of trees, bushes, palms, creepers and cedars often draped with grey Spanish moss and home to many flowering airplants.

The tour returned along the Hontoon Dead River back to Hontoon Landing, concluding what is aptly described as "a most beautiful cruise in the St Johns River Valley."

Cost
Adults $22 with concessions for seniors and children

Tour Times
Tours take place daily at 10 a.m. and 1 p.m.

Where to Eat in DeLand
DeLand has plenty of locally owned coffee shops and cafés. The Boston Coffeehouse on E. New York Ave is a great place for breakfast or lunch.

Mainstreet Grill is popular with locals and has a nice outdoor patio area. Try the Black and Blue Wedge Salad or the Cordon Bleu Chicken for something tasty and a little unusual.

Nearby Attractions
- Deleon Springs State Park
- Central Florida Zoo, Sanford
- DeBary Hall

Swim with Manatees in the Crystal River

This eco-friendly adventure is a thrilling experience for all ages as you interact with wild manatees in the clear water of the Crystal River and Kings Bay Manatee Refuge. This unique spring-fed ecosystem is the only place in the world where you can actually swim and interact face-to-face with the docile manatees you will encounter.

Trips include a boat ride in search of these gentle giants as well as snorkel equipment and wetsuits.

Crystal River Ventures is one of only a few regulated companies with a special license allowing them to offer "passive observation" tours with manatees. The boat captains are all USCG licensed masters and they demonstrate a caring and responsible attitude in ensuring the well-being of these endangered creatures.

The trained Manatee Tour Guides accompany you into the water. They provide full instruction before the trip along with plenty of information about manatees, making it a very educational fun experience.

This thrilling trip is suitable for first-time snorkelers and anyone over the age of 2 years. For those who don't want to get into the water, you can view the manatees clearly from the boat. In my opinion this is one of the best days out you could possibly have with your grandkids!

Location
Located at Crystal River just off US-19/98 (N. Suncoast Blvd) 42 miles east of The Villages.

Crystal River Ventures
498 SE Kings Bay Drive
Crystal River
FL34429
Tel: (352) 564-8687 or (877) 581-8401

www.riverventures.com

What to Expect on a Crystal River Manatee Tour
The warm spring-fed waters of the Crystal River are one of the best places in Florida to see manatees all year round. This is also the only area in the world that is licensed for interactive tours with manatees, which are an endangered species.

Swimming with manatees is an exhilarating experience as you interact with these docile giants in their own natural habitat.

Manatees are similar to seals with a huge gray body and thick skin. They can reach up to 13 feet in length and weigh over 3,000 pounds yet they are totally non-aggressive. They spend their time moving slowly up and down the Crystal River grazing on seagrass.

Manatees need warm water to survive and consequently the winter months are the best time to see them in large numbers in the Crystal River National Wildlife Refuge. They congregate in the 72°F spring waters, particularly on cold nights. The best time to swim with them is on the early morning tour before the river becomes busy with boat traffic and other tours.

On arrival at Crystal River Ventures, check in at the tour center and enjoy a complimentary drink as you watch an informative video about how to snorkel and interact with manatees. There are certain rules regarding swimming with manatees which generally require you to treat these wild animals with respect. Expect your tour to last for around three hours.

You'll be fitted for a wetsuit and given a snorkel, fins and mask so you need to arrive 10-15 minutes ahead of your tour departure time. Once everyone is ready, board the pontoon boat and you're off! There are plenty of seats for everyone for the ride out to meet the manatees. The boats are equipped with a porta-potty behind a curtained area for emergencies.

The guide gives lots of information about manatees and what to expect on your trip. You can feel the excitement in the air as everyone keeps an eye open looking for groups of grey manatees in the water. First signs are usually when they surface and put their whiskery nose above the water to breathe. Fortunately the spring waters are so clear you can spot them from quite a distance away against the white limestone riverbed.

Once the boatmaster has chosen a spot, he cuts the engine and drifts into the area near the manatees. Snorkelers quietly enter the water accompanied by the guide who will ensure a safe and enjoyable experience for both swimmers and manatees.

Once you are floating in the water, the manatees will slowly approach as they are naturally curious, playful and friendly. It is an amazing experience as they drift closer to check you out. If you're lucky you'll see Moms with their calves and you'll be able to give them a stroke.

Gillian Birch

Time seems to go by so fast as you snorkel and interact with the manatees. Of course there are plenty of other fish in the river to spot and identify too. You can get in and out of the water as often as you like during this magical trip.

There is a private curtained area to change onboard after the final swim or you can use the changing rooms back at the tour center. On the return journey the boat is full of happy chatter as everyone recalls their favorite moments of this thrilling wildlife experience.

Additional Information
Wear a swimsuit underneath your regular clothes to make changing quick and easy, and bring a towel. It's a good idea to buy a disposable underwater camera or get a special underwater camera bag so you can take great underwater photos of your family swimming with the manatees.

The trip includes some official photos taken by your guide which you can buy on a CD. You will definitely want a photo souvenir of this incredible swimming with manatees experience!

The trip is suitable for anyone who is comfortable in the water, from 2 years of age to seniors. Nervous swimmers can request an inflatable vest or foam noodle for added buoyancy. Children under 18 must be accompanied by an adult.

Admission
All inclusive cost $45 per person.

Opening Times

Swimming with Manatee Tours are available daily excluding Thanksgiving and Christmas.

Tours are offered at 6.15 a.m., 9.15 a.m. and additionally at 12.15 p.m. in colder months.

Where to Eat at Crystal River

Of course everyone will be ravenous after being in the water and there's a huge choice of good places to eat in Crystal River.

One place to rave about is the Seafood Seller Café at the Crystal River Mall near K-Mart. They open at noon and do some surprisingly good New Orleans style seafood dishes and steaks at reasonable prices. You won't be disappointed here.

The Highlander Café on N. Citrus Ave is a popular brunch place for locals and is open until 3pm, or try Cody's Roadhouse on Hwy 19 which is very family friendly - and you get peanuts while you wait!

Nearby Attractions
- Three Sisters Spring and Boardwalk
- Cooter Pond Park and Boardwalk, Inverness
- Homosassa Springs Wildlife State Park

Indoor Skydiving at iFLY

If you fancy all the thrills of skydiving without the expense or the risk, indoor skydiving is definitely for you! iFLY Orlando offers the chance to fly in a vertical wind tunnel one-on-one with a professional instructor. Suitable for all ages from 3 up, the package includes training, flight gear and two flights.

Location
Just off International Drive Orlando, opposite Wet 'n'Wild

iFLY Indoor Skydiving
6805 Visitors Circle
Orlando, FL32819
Tel: (407) 903-1150

https://orlando.iflyworld.com/

What to Expect at iFLY

On arrival at the iFLY building, check-in is airport style at individual computer screens. Flyers have to sign a waiver before receiving a wristband.

This is the time to book a photo CD and video of your flight. Having done it myself, the flight experience is fantastic, but it passes like a blur as you are concentrating on keeping airborne and enjoying the thrill. A video of your flight enables you see yourself afterwards and re-live the whole experience as well as being able to share it with the rest of the family. Pre-ordering a video is definitely recommended to make the most of your flight.

After check-in, flyers and spectators climb the metal staircase and enter the observation room. Flights are usually in progress and you get your first taste of what you and your family are about to experience. Bench seats are arranged around one side of the flying chamber, which has windows on all sides and a mesh floor.

You will see other fliers launch themselves into the air with the instructor and fly around the chamber. More experienced fliers may be doing stunts and flips, learning to stand, or flying on their backs and fronts. Highly experienced groups can make it all look incredibly easy!

Your instructor will collect your group of about 12 flyers and take you to the briefing room to explain the flight position. As first-time flyers you are likely to be flying on your front, chin up, arms out, legs straight and keeping a curved back. You will also learn the hand signals to give and expect and any questions will be answered.

Next you will be given appropriately sized flying suits, earplugs, goggles and a helmet. Lockers are provided for personal items and all loose jewelry should be removed and stowed safely.

You will then be taken to the flying chamber, on the opposite side to the spectators, where you can squeeze onto the platform in the launch area. The huge wind turbines start up to generate wind speeds of over 100mph. A controller will match the air velocity and volume to each flyer.

Flying is easy. When your turn comes simply step through the doorway into the wind tunnel, lean into the wind and take off. The instructor constantly steadies and monitors each person individually. As you begin to gain confidence, you will find yourself flying around unaided in the wind tunnel. The instructor gives hand signals for chin up, straight legs or whatever is required.

All too soon the minute is over and you grab the doorframe and pull yourself out onto the landing platform. There are likely to be broad smiles, high-fives and thumbs up from the group, adding to the sense of achievement and camaraderie.

The second flight is much the same, although those who are confident can fly high up into the chimney with the instructor for a real sense of height and speed. At the end of the flight, the instructor spends a minute showing what the experts can do, bouncing expertly off the walls, flipping, rising and descending in an amazing demonstration of skill.

All too soon the experience is over and everyone troops back to the briefing area to change and receive their souvenir flight certificate. It is a truly brilliant experience in a totally safe, controlled environment with constant attention from trained instructors who work incredibly hard to give everyone a thrilling flight.

Additional Info

The total experience lasts about an hour. There are two flights, each lasting about one minute.

The video is definitely worth the extra money so you get to see yourself in action and recall this amazing experience.

No previous experience is necessary and anyone can enjoy a body flight, from aged 3 upwards.

Wear comfortable clothing such as jeans or trousers and trainers or suitable footwear.

Admission

Training, equipment and two one-minute flights for beginners package is $59.95 per person. Various other packages are available for families and those with prior iFLY experience.

Advance reservations are recommended as iFLY can get booked up, especially on busy weekends.

Opening Times
Open daily 10 a.m. to 10 p.m.

Where to Eat around iFLY
iFLY Orlando is just off International Drive. There is a wide choice of fast food outlets, restaurants and pizza parlors nearby including Pie-Fection on S. Kirkman Road where you can build your own pizza from the sauce up.

While you are in Orlando you may want to book places at the Medieval Times Dinner Show which includes a meal and jousting entertainment in one of the best dinner shows in Florida.

Nearby Attractions
- Ripley's Believe It or Not!
- Wet 'n Wild
- Medieval Times

Gatorland

If you want to do something completely different, take the grandkids down to Gatorland on S. Orange Blossom Trail (US 17/441). I was so impressed on my afternoon visit that I would have gone there sooner had I known just how much it had to offer!

As well as the expected pools of alligators, there is a veritable zoo of animals, from emus and giant tortoises to flamingoes, owls, parrots and deer. There is also a petting zoo, boardwalk, train ride, fantastic Screamin' Gator zip line adventure, splashzone and three excellent animal shows. It's the perfect day out for families of all ages.

Location

Located on Hwy 441 in South Orlando, just 15 minutes from Walt Disney World

Gatorland
14501 S. Orange Blossom Trail
Orlando
FL32837
Tel: (407) 855-5496 or (800) 393-5297

http://www.gatorland.com/

What to Expect on a Visit to Gatorland

Newly rebuilt in 2008, the park at Gatorland is nicely laid out and everything is attractive and well-kept. Your first photo opportunity will be at the entrance where there is a giant alligator jaw which you walk through to enter.

After visiting the large gift shop and ticket office, which has walls plastered with archive images of the park, you come to two large lakes which seem to be a mass of alligator bodies. There are different sized gators and crocodiles in various other pools too. The lakes are actually big enough to have islands and one is home to a colony of pretty pink flamingos. Kids will enjoy buying some special food and throwing it to the alligators to see their snapping jaws.

Along the main drag there are a series of animal exhibits in outdoor displays or aquariums. Look out for sandhill cranes, Burmese pythons, a truly giant tortoise and a wide range of other snakes, animals and birds in cornily named areas such as the Very Merry Aviary and Allie's Barnyard. The nice surprise is that visitors can go into the pen and touch/stroke the animals and even handle the colorful lorikeets that fly down for food. The snakes, fortunately, were well secured behind glass.

After riding around the park on the Choo-Choo Express, head for the long raised boardwalk through the native Cypress Swamp. It's a really nice area to amble along beside a naturalized lake area. This is the Breeding Marsh and Bird Rookery where 130 adult gators live in the 10-acre wetland environment. Everywhere you look you will see alligator eyes unblinkingly staring at you. The accompanying fact boards do a good job of informing you of the breeding habits of alligators, and actual identify some of the reptiles by their territory, size or individual characteristics.

Daring visitors can climb the Observation Tower and clip their harness to the Screamin' Gator Zipline under careful instruction from the trainer. Then you're off, flying high above the greenery and water as you go from platform to platform.

The Splash Zone is a great place for youngsters to cool off with many jets, flumes and water features.

It's worth hanging around for the last show of the day, the Gator Jumparoo Show. The alligators circle in the water, clearly knowing food is due. Eventually they jump high into the area to snap at a whole chicken. They make quite a splash!

The other excellent shows which take place throughout the day include Gator Wrestling, where wranglers do a series of stunts, and there's an Upclose Encounters Show where some of Florida's oddest creatures are displayed and talked about by trained staff.

All-in-all Gatorland is a really enjoyable attraction that I can highly recommend to families of all ages.

Additional Info
Parking at the attraction is free.

Additional events at Gatorland include the Gator Night Shine after dark, or sign up and become a Trainer for a Day.

Admission
Adults $26.99 for a day pass with concessions for children aged 3-12.

Opening Times
Open daily 10 a.m. to 5 p.m.

Where to Eat At Gatorland
There is affordable hot food at Pearl's Smokehouse in Gatorland including burgers, pulled pork sandwiches and even fried gator nuggets! There's also a general store and a coffee shop onsite.

Alternatively, bring a picnic and make use of the attraction's picnic tables.

Nearby Attractions
- Ripley's Believe It or Not!
- iFLY Orlando
- Boggy Creek Airboat Rides Kissimmee

Florida Museum of Natural History and Butterfly Rainforest

Located on the University of Florida University campus in Gainesville, the Florida Museum of Natural History is one of the top five natural history museums in the U.S. Most of the permanent exhibitions are free to visit and include an award-winning exhibit of Florida fossils, butterflies and insects, a Waterways and Wildlife exhibit, a recreated limestone cave and a boardwalk through a mangrove forest to the home of a native Calusa Indian leader.

The separate Butterfly Rainforest is a truly outstanding experience. The screened enclosure contains a rainforest setting with waterfalls, boardwalks, tropical plants and flowers that are home to thousands of brightly colored butterflies. Watching these exotic creatures fluttering from plant to plant as they feed on nectar makes this a truly mesmerizing attraction for all generations.

Location

Located on the University of Florida campus one mile east of I-75 Exit 384.

Florida Museum of Natural History
Powell Hall
3215 Hull Road
Gainesville
FL32611
Tel: (352) 846-2000

www.flmnh.ufl.edu

What to Expect on a Visit to the Florida Museum of Natural History

The Florida Museum of Natural History has everything you need for a family-friendly day out. Rather than dry and boring exhibits behind glass, the Florida Museum of Natural History is light and bright with plenty of touchy-feely exhibits and areas for families to explore and discover together.

Although most of the exhibition areas are free to visit, you need to purchase tickets when you arrive at the Front Desk if you intend to visit the temporary exhibits or the Butterfly Rainforest.

You'll be greeted at the door by the 14-foot high skeleton of a tusked Columbian Mammoth, said to be over 16,000 years old. It was discovered in the Aucilla River in northwest Florida where the remains of this now extinct creature had been fossilized and preserved.

There are plenty of hands-on activities throughout the attraction such as the Discovery Room in the Children's Gallery which is designed to stimulate and encourage natural curiosity. There's a fossil dig in sand and many other activities to try your hand at.

Other areas of the Florida Museum have "secret" drawers for children to pull out and examine the colorful collections of insects and wildlife. You'll find objects from archaeological digs, fossils, seashells, teeth and even the skull of Albert, one of the first live alligator mascots that belonged to the university!

Further along the Central Gallery you can visit the Waterways and Wildlife display of Northwest Florida. Follow the flowing waterways and discover some of the strange creatures that lurk beneath logs in the hardwood hammocks. You may even spot an American Crocodile!

The recreated limestone cave is another popular area for families. You can walk through the cave, and see the various natural formations and discover the creatures that spend their lives entirely in the dark.

Further along is the South Florida People and Environments Room. Follow the story of the indigenous people of Florida and how they lived in this hostile environment. The exhibit includes a boardwalk through the mangroves, the chance to witness a Calusa Indian Welcome Ceremony and you can travel underwater to see many unusual marine creatures that are part of our Florida heritage. Another display features a natural seepage bog with strange carnivorous plants that trap insects in their traps and pitchers.

The recreated Native American trading scene, outdoor shell mound and wildlife exhibits are accompanied by the sound effects of birdsong, frogs and crickets, making it very atmospheric.

The Hall of Florida Fossils is a display of evolution. Covering over 65 million years of prehistory, the exhibit shows the past diversity of life in Florida including a jaguar, bear dog, giant sloths and ferocious terror birds.

At the far end of the West Gallery are a series of viewing windows where visitors can see into the labs and watch scientists working on the various natural history collections and research projects.

As well as the permanent exhibitions listed, there are temporary exhibits which change regularly. Past themes have included the Megalodon – the largest shark that ever lived; Chocolate; Wolf to Woof, the evolutionary story of dogs, and the dinosaur exhibit of Sue, a 42-foot long skeleton of a Tyrannosaurus Rex.

Butterfly Rainforest

One section of the Florida Museum is dedicated to Butterflies. The McGuire Center is the world's largest facility dedicated to the study of global butterflies and moths (lepidoptera). It houses one of the largest collections of butterflies and the amazing "Wall of Wings" shows thousands of different species carefully preserved as a record of the diversity of moth and butterfly biology.

Take time to look at the butterfly eggs (pupae) laid out by scientists on sticky paper in the rearing lab. The eggs are kept in warm moist conditions and there are usually at least a couple of eggs hatching. You can see newly emerged butterflies drying their wings before they are released into the Butterfly Rainforest. It's well worth spending time in this area and reading the information boards before moving into the Butterfly Rainforest itself.

There is a charge for the Butterfly Rainforest area but in my opinion it is the highlight of the visit. Once you have been checked through security you can enter this 6,400 square-foot outdoor screened atrium of rainforest plants, flowers and gorgeous butterflies. Pick up a butterfly identifying card to make the most of your experience.

Your eyes will quickly start spotting the colorful movements of butterflies everywhere. Bright blue, orange, yellow, multicolored and iridescent butterflies are everywhere in this lush oasis. There are between 60-80 species of butterflies and moths of all sizes and shapes in this breathtaking setting.

Waterfalls and pools are home to turtles, fish and exotic birds that can live in harmony with the main stars – the tropical butterflies.

Everyone becomes entranced by the beautiful setting and you will see youngsters peering at resting butterflies while adults point out one gorgeous species after another as they flit between the greenery. It's also a great photo opportunity, so have your camera ready to capture some great family photos as a memento of your visit.

The Butterfly Rainforest leads you back to the entrance foyer but there are a couple more things to see before leaving. There is a Collector's Gift Shop near the entrance in addition to the gorgeous butterfly-themed Gift Shop near the Butterfly Rainforest. Proceeds help support the work of this beautiful museum, allowing admission to remain largely free.

Outside the museum there is a Fossil Plant Garden and a demonstration garden of Florida's wildflowers and butterfly host plants. There's also a Plant Sale area if you want to buy a plant to attract butterflies to your Florida garden in The Villages.

Additional Information

Cameras and camcorders are welcome for personal use in the museum and Butterfly Rainforest.

No food, drinks, tobacco or gum are permitted in the museum, particularly in the Butterfly Rainforest where they could be harmful to the butterflies. For security, all bags must be checked in at the desk before entering the Butterfly Rainforest.

Parking costs $4 per day Monday to Friday. It is free after 3.30 p.m. on weekdays, free on weekends and during public and university holidays.

Admission
Many exhibits in the Florida Museum of Natural History are free to visit. There are charges for some visiting temporary exhibitions.

Admission to the Butterfly Rainforest is $10.50 for adults and $6 for children aged 3-17. There are concessions for Florida residents and seniors.

Opening Times
Open Monday – Saturday 10 a.m. to 5 p.m.; Sunday 1-5 p.m.

Closed Thanksgiving and Christmas.

Where to Eat at the Florida Museum
There is a covered outdoor picnic area with seats and tables if you want to enjoy snacks or a picnic lunch as part of your visit.

Alternatively, head into Gainesville and enjoy the ultimate pizza buffet at SteviB's on NW 13th Street. Grandparents are allowed to indulge in unhealthy treats now and then!

Nearby Attractions
- Carson Springs Wildlife Conservation
- Kanapaha Botanical Gardens
- Two Tails Ranch, Williston

Carson Springs Wildlife Conservation Foundation

Florida is known for its wildlife, but when you take the family to Carson Springs you'll encounter lions, tigers and leopards along with giraffes, oryx, jackals and cute red lemurs. This beautiful animal conservation sanctuary shares the extensive 274-acre horse facility with animals straight from Africa, Madagascar and other exotic destinations.

This fabulous wildlife conservation foundation is so much more than a zoo. Many of the 80 animals that now consider Carson Springs their home come from attractions where they are used for cute photographs as babies – a career they quickly outgrow. Other animals are rescue animals or former pets whose owners can no longer keep them, either due to personal circumstances or due to the recent changes in the law which now prohibit ownership of certain pets without a federal license. Carson Springs is also a breeding facility for many endangered animals, including some that are actually extinct in the wild.

The enthusiasm and dedication of the staff and the chance to get up close and interact with many of the animals makes this a thrilling animal experience for both adults and youngsters.

Location
Located 17 miles northeast of Gainesville towards Starke.

Carson Springs Wildlife Conservation
8528 E. County Road 225
Gainesville
FL32609
Tel: (352) 468-2827

http://www.carsonspringswildlife.org

What to Expect on a Visit to Carson Springs
You need to make a prior reservation in order to access the gates and security into Carson Springs.

Every visitor joins a guided tour with a wildlife specialist who makes the visit particularly informative and personal. Far from being a restrictive tour, there's plenty of space for children to run around on the broad grass pathways. In fact they are encouraged to do so as the big cats love to join in and play chase or stalk them – from behind the safety of a double fence, of course!

The two-hour tour of the wildlife sanctuary starts and finishes at the gift shop and picnic area where you can appreciate the enormous scale of the sanctuary and how well-maintained it is. This reflects in the many animals you will see that all seem happy in their spacious green landscaped areas which far exceed the requirements laid down by the state.

One thing I particularly noticed was that the animals were lively, curious and inquisitive. They approached the fence to greet the owner, Christine, and manager/tour guide Nicole as they escort visitors around the sanctuary. The tigers certainly wanted to "chuff" and communicate as you approach to admire their beautiful markings and gorgeous coats.

The tour takes you over areas of neatly mown grass which are dotted with many established trees as you move from one enclosure to the next.

Visitors of all ages are enchanted by the rare opportunity to come face to face with many exotic animals that you are unlikely to encounter in their native habitat. Hyenas, jackals, sitanagas, giraffes, cougars, lions, tigers, several species of shy lemurs, pointy-eared caracals, owls, emus and even giant tortoises are all introduced as you work your way around the sanctuary, delighting in each new creature. It's an educational experience for all generations!

All the animals are named so you'll get to meet Gaby the tiger, Savannah the jackal, Massey the lynx, Ed and Leah the lions and many more.

Some of the fences have informative signs telling you more about the residents. Three of the stars are Koko, Kela and Misha, the large tigers whose agility and playfulness belie their age. Koko is now 13 but with a life expectancy of at least 20 years, she has plenty more happy years ahead of her at this beautiful facility. The tigers even have their own pool for cooling off in!

Listen out for all the different noises as you follow the tour. You'll hear dog-like barks from the oryx (which incidentally are now extinct in the wild), purrs and meows from the handsome cheetahs and a noisy racket coming from the tiny lemurs if they want to show their disapproval of their neighbors!

Some of the rare and endangered species that are being cared for at Carson Springs include Siberian lynx and Asian Fishing Cats which are now endangered in the wild.

As you can imagine, all kids love animal encounters, but at Carson Springs the animals also appear to love kids! They will follow along watching, rubbing the fences with their faces as a sign of communication. The sight of the animals chasing up and down beside excited children is so surprising and amusing to watch.

Touching and stroking most of the animals is obviously out of the question, but youngsters do get the chance to handle and touch the tortoises in their grassy pen.

Everyone is encouraged to ask questions so you will learn that the sanctuary needs around 100 pounds of raw meat per day which is a huge and expensive undertaking. Your admission fees, donations and sponsorship all go to ensuring the animals are probably fed and cared for.

Volunteers are a vital part of keeping this sanctuary spotlessly clean and the animals well cared for. Veterinary services and meds can eat into the budget of this fully licensed non-profit organization, but local vets from "All Cats" generously donate their time.

Back at the gift shop, the building houses cages, restrooms and a maternity room for breeding some of the rare animals before delivering them to other zoos and animal facilities across the United States. You may even see some of the newest arrivals if you are very lucky.

Carson Springs is such a different day out for grandparents and children compared to a traditional zoo, which is why I just had to include it in this book. It offers the unique chance to get up close to the animals, interact with them and listen to their noisy responses.

The peaceful setting of this beautifully maintained ranch makes this a truly memorable visit that I would definitely urge you to make.

Tours Costs
Tours are by donation - $25 for adults and $5 for children.

Reservations are essential.

Opening Times
Tour times by prior arrangement.

Where to Eat near Carson Springs

Gainesville has a good choice of places to dine, about 17 miles away. My personal favorite is Harry's Seafood Bar and Grille which serves great New Orleans style cuisine on SE 1st Street.

There are also several chain fast food outlets in Williston including Subway, KFC and Hardees.

Nearby Attractions

- Marjorie Kinnan Rawlings Historic State Park
- Two Tails Ranch, Williston
- Florida Museum and Butterfly Rainforest
- Kanapaha Botanical Gardens

Marine Discovery Center in New Smyrna Beach

Combine a day at the beach with a visit to the Marine Discovery Center. It's a real hidden gem, particularly for those wanting to amuse grandchildren with supervised and educational activities. The Science Center has daily activities such as oyster recycling, crafts and fishing so it's well worth booking ahead and joining in the fun.

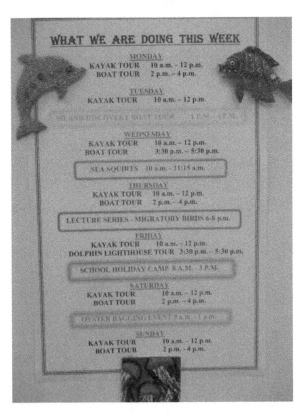

Hop aboard one of the daily boat trips, dolphin tours, guided kayak tours and hands-on adventure tours all led by certified naturalists. Book ahead or just drop into the Marine Discovery Center any time and have fun exploring the free exhibits and touch tanks. You'll certainly want to come back for more!

Location
Located on the Indian River Lagoon just north of Hwy 44.

Marine Discovery Center (MDC)
520 Barracuda Blvd
New Smyrna Beach
FL32169
Tel: (386) 428-4828

www.marinediscoverycenter.org

What to Expect on a Visit to the Marine Discovery Center
The Marine Discovery Center is a wonderful reason to visit New Smyrna Beach in conjunction with a trip to the beautiful sandy beach which you can actually drive on and park for a nominal fee.

The Marine Discovery Center is a fun place to drop in and look around for free with various observation tanks containing hermit crabs in large conch shells, horseshoe crabs semi buried in the sand, and crown conch.

Children are encouraged to pull out the drawer displays and discover sea shells, sea beans, shark's skin and other curious exhibits. A display of shark's teeth is certainly fascinating, along with the huge teeth of the extinct megalodon and other extinct sea creatures.

Even more fun are the many tanks of sea creatures at the center. There are aquariums of pretty starfish, anemones, fish, crabs and other unusual sea creatures.

When we visited, my grandchildren loved the sea horses that were nosing around in seaweed. The docent told us they were due to give birth and the tiny babies are born fully formed and well able to fend for themselves.

The rear classroom has more to see, from colorful posters on the wall to skulls, a corn snake, an interesting shark tank and more fish. This room is used for many activities which are suitable for all ages.

The Marine Discovery Center offers 2-hour Dolphin Discovery Tours daily on a pontoon boat to see dolphins, manatees and birds in their natural habitat. There are also daily guided kayak tours with a marine specialist guide who will take you through the mangroves and backwaters for close encounters with local wildlife.

If you want to get more hands-on, the excellent Island Adventure Tours take place on the first and third Tuesday of the month. These 3-hour interactive eco tours are led by certified naturalists.

With the help of sieves, dip and seine nets (and wet feet!) guests find and identify fish, conchs, sea stars, horseshoe crabs and other wildlife around the islands and sandbars of the Indian River.

Additional Info
The Marine Discovery Center is within easy reach of the charming shops, cafés, art galleries and businesses in Flagler Ave's historic homes and the Old Seaside Station.

Admission
Admission to the center and its touch tank exhibits is free.

Dolphin Discovery Tours (2 hours)
Adults $25

Seniors and Students $22

Children under 12 $10.

Family ticket for 2 adults and 2 children $60.

Guided Kayak Tours (2 hours)
Adults $30

Children 6-12 $20

Island Adventure Tours (3 hours hands-on)
Adults $30

Seniors $27

Children under 12 $15

Opening Times
The Marine Discovery Center and Gift Shop is open daily 9 a.m. to 5 p.m.

Where to Eat At New Smyrna Beach

Browse the cafés and restaurants on historic Flagler Ave nearby or head out to the beach on Atlantic Ave.

One of my favorite places is Breakers which is right on the beach on S. Atlantic Ave. There are plenty of outdoor tables so you can keep an eye on the children as they run off their energy on the firm sands or play in the tidal pools. It's very casual and family friendly with generous portions and decent food.

Nearby Attractions

- Blue Spring State Park
- Sun Splash Park, Daytona
- Daytona International Speedway Museum and Track Tours

Dinosaur World

Most youngsters speak fluent "dinosaur" and the prehistoric world of dinosaurs never fails to capture their imagination. Dinosaur World is a fascinating place to visit, allowing visitors to learn more about these prehistoric giants through fossils, models and a variety of hands-on activities and shows.

This dinosaur-themed attraction includes the world's largest collection of life-size dinosaurs set in a pleasant woodland park setting. The range of activities, educational facts, museum of fossilized dinosaur remains and the huge prehistoric models make this attraction far more interesting and scientific than I could ever have imagined.

The reasonably priced admission includes free parking, over 200 life-size dinosaurs, a Fossil Dig where each child can take home their favorite finds, a Dino Gem excavation where you can sift paydirt for gems and arrowheads, a comprehensive Prehistoric Museum, giant wooly mammoths, a life-size Tyrannosaurus Rex skull in the Skeleton Garden, and many other outdoor exhibits.

Grandparents, prepare to be as enthralled as the youngsters on your visit to Dinosaur World!

Location
Located in Plant City between Orlando and Tampa on I-4 Exit 17.

Dinosaur World
5145 Harvey Tew Road
Plant City
FL335565
Tel: (813) 717-9865

www.dinosaurworld.com/

What to Expect on a Visit to Dinosaur World
Start your visit to Dinosaur World in the huge gift shop and welcome center where you can purchase tickets and pick up a map of the 20-acre theme park.

First stop after taking in the initial dinosaur models is the Prehistoric Museum which is a great introduction to paleontology, the study of fossils and once-living organisms.

The museum has many fascinating fossils, ammonites and genuine dinosaur eggs. The sound effects make it particularly impressive as you step back in time and see claws of long extinct mammals, the tooth of a spinosaurus, mammoth tusks and teeth and the ginormous clawed foot, toes and dewclaw of an allosaurus dating back to the Jurassic period.

Back outside, follow the paths and boardwalks around the lovely park setting admiring the dinosaur models, some of which move and squawk, so be warned!

The grounds are well-maintained with lawned areas, tall trees, woods and a river running through. It makes the perfect setting for dinosaur models that suddenly appear in the greenery. Enjoy the birds, feed the koi in the pond and watch squirrels foraging for food in this eco-friendly setting.

The boardwalks and paths lead through different groups of dinosaurs from carnivores and raptors to plant-eating giants. Their fierce-looking horns, teeth, claws, bills, body plates and tail spikes clearly made them very well armored.

Storyboards show that discoveries of dinosaur remains have been found in Wyoming, Colorado, Utah, Canada, Africa and Europe.

Throughout Dinosaur World there are interactive games, play areas, touch and tell exhibits, information boards with bite-size facts and many different interpretations of the dinosaur era to keep everyone entertained.

You can explore the Skeleton Garden or discover stegosaurus skeleton parts in the boneyard where would-be paleontologists can carefully clean their finds with a paintbrush.

There are various timed activities and games throughout the day including an excellent Cave Show where paleontologists "find" dinosaur bones and follow the process to discover the age and provenance of each prehistoric find.

Fossils, Geodes and Gems

As you explore the attraction you will pass the Fossil Dig which is a fun area for youngsters to unearth some genuine fossils to take home. Sifting the sand will reveal genuine shark teeth, stingray barbs, mosasaur teeth and various fossils which the attendant will help identify. Children can bag up their favorite three finds to take home as an interesting souvenir.

Another fun activity is the Dino Gem Mine where you receive a bucket of fossilized coprolite and dirt containing dinosaur bones, minerals and semi-precious stones such as amethysts and citrines. The running water in the sluice allows you to wash away the dirt and discover your glittering take-home treasures.

There is also a Geode Cracker where enthusiastic rock hounds can crack open geodes (bumpy spherical rocks lined with crystalline) and discover the fantastic crystal formations of quartz and Keokuk inside. Like dinosaurs, these rock formations are all millions of years old.

Admission to the Park

Adults $16.95 with concessions for seniors ($14.95) and children 3-12 ($11.95)

Excavation Pass (which includes admission, Fossil Dig, Dino Gem Excavation and fish food)

Adults $22.75; Children $18.95

Opening Times

Open daily 9 a.m. to 5 p.m.

Where to Eat at Dinosaur World

There is no restaurant at Dinosaur World but it's a great place to enjoy a picnic in one of the covered picnic areas.

Pick up lunch from Publix Deli or Subway on the journey and dine with the dinosaurs – you'll save on lunch costs too!

Nearby Attractions

- Florida Aquarium
- Glazer Children's Museum
- Lowry Park Zoo

Glazer Children's Museum

Forget dull and boring, the Glazer Children's Museum in Tampa is all about children (and their grandparents!) having fun and playing while learning how things work. This incredible museum has plenty of activities spread over three floors that will stretch the imagination, inspire experimentation and encourage children to be whatever they want to be, from a firefighter to a TV weather reporter!

The museum is ideally designed for accompanied children from toddlers to 10 years old. As well as being a drop-in attraction, the museum also offers half day and full day themed camps during school holidays in association with the YMCA.

There are currently 17 exhibit galleries that explore topics such as water, weather, sport and flight. Activities take place in a modern, safe environment with staff available to assist and demonstrate. This superb museum attraction even has an on-site Subway, so you really can stay all day!

Location
Located in downtown Tampa next to the Tampa Museum of Art on the Riverwalk.

Glazer Children's Museum
110 W. Gasparilla Plaza
Tampa
FL33602
Tel: (813) 443-3861

http://glazermuseum.org

What to Expect on a Visit to the Glazer Children's Museum
Pick up a map at the Visitor Services as you enter this fabulous world of discovery through play. First stop will probably be the KidsPort where a flowing river invites kids to make dams, make waves and experiment with tug boats, cargo cranes and pulleys.

Water play includes turning wheels for water flow, operating paddles, watching boat races and operating an Archimedes Screw to carry water up to feed a waterwheel. If you're worried about the kids getting wet before the day has barely begun, there are cute sets of oilskins for them to wear.

Older children will be fascinated by the Rain or Shine weather creator. Choose three buttons such as rain, wind and thunder and hey-presto – the clouds above generate real wind, fine rain, lightning flashes and noisy thunder to order!

Under 4s will enjoy the Tugboat Tots, complete with ship's wheel, levers to pull and buttons to press. There's a sand corner for barefoot play in the Cruise Ship area. Every activity has an educational aspect and adults will be as engrossed as the kids they are accompanying!

Suspended above the sand play is the Water's Journey – a series of raindrop-shaped platforms in scramble nets which older children can safely scramble up and through to quite a height.

On the second floor there's plenty more to keep everyone happily occupied in the Art Smart Lab. Visit the interactive Sports Corner where you can race an animal or be the goalie and see yourself in action on the live screen.

Some of the high-tech media activities are sponsored by Bay News 9, Bright House Networks and Telemundo Tampa. One of their amazing exhibits is the chance to do a local weather report "live" on TV reading from a teleprompter. Kids will certainly enjoying seeing themselves on TV!

A series of exhibits offer role play opportunities for children. They can pilot a plane complete with uniforms, hats and virtual cockpit screens.

Further along the gallery, the Design and Build has everything you need to be a plumber, builder or crane operator. The City of Play Pretend includes a mini-Publix with shelves stocked with groceries and checkout scanners. There's also a veterinary clinic with plenty of cuddly animals to x-ray and treat, a hospital, Central Bank and a Firehouse with pole, fire engine and all the gear.

We're not done yet! Little engineers can construct the perfect paper airplane with the help of museum educators then test fly it in the wind tunnel.

Special daily events take place in the My House, Your House Theater, including hands-on cookery programs. While whipping up a dessert, kids can learn about cuisine and cultures in other countries. The Twinkle Theater has lights, sound effects, costumes, curtains and props for groups to produce their own drama.

If you stay until 4.30 p.m. you can join in the end-of-day parade with songs and dancing led by the imaginative museum staff. Your grandkids probably won't allow you to leave without visiting the Museum Gift Store which has some excellent educational games, toys and projects.

New plans for the Children's Museum in 2015 include an extensive walk-in Wizard of Oz exhibit on the third floor.

Additional Information

Winter visitors can combine the museum with the pop-up ice rink which is erected right next to the museum from late November through early January.

Admission to the Museum
Adults $15, children age 1-12 $9.50

Opening Times
Open Monday to Friday 10 a.m. to 5 p.m., Saturday 10 a.m. to 6 p.m. and Sunday 1-6 p.m.

Closed on most major holidays.

Where to Eat at the Glazer Children's Museum
There is a Subway on the ground floor of the museum near the excellent gift shop.

Older children and fans of the TV program *Diners, Drive-Ins and Dives* may want to visit Danny's All American Diner and Dairy Bar on N. Falkenburg Rd which is about 15 minutes' drive from the Aquarium. Most first time visitors want to try the Guy Fieri Triple D Triple Play – a meat overload of Mojo pork, pastrami, Swiss cheese, tomatoes, mustard, jalapeno peppers and fried onion rings on grilled sourdough bread. However, the Danny's Hot Dogs, Philly Cheesesteak, Cuban sandwiches and vast choice of tasty specials are pretty awesome too. It certainly makes the journey to Tampa worthwhile!

Nearby Attractions
- Lowry Park Zoo
- Florida Aquarium
- Giraffe Ranch
- Dinosaur World

Florida Aquarium

The Florida Aquarium in Tampa is one of the top aquariums in the U.S., and once you've visited you will appreciate why. It is a huge and spacious attraction with over 1600 fish, sharks, stingrays and sea turtles as well as some unexpected exhibits such as penguins, gators, waterbirds, a "no-bone zone" and a 2-acre outdoor Explore-a-Shore water play area.

Daily highlights at this world-class attraction include live animal presentations, a splendid Q&A session with a submerged diver in the vast 250,000 square-foot aquarium, otter feeding, and presentations at the panoramic viewing window. If you want to add a special experience, perhaps as a birthday treat, there are exciting opportunities including behind-the-scenes tours, hands-on feeding activities and swimming with the fish!

Location

Located 1.6 miles south of I-275 Exit 45A (Downtown East Jefferson St) in downtown Tampa.

Florida Aquarium
701 Channelside Drive
Tampa
FL33602
Tel: (813) 273-4000

www.flaquarium.org

What to Expect on a Visit to the Florida Aquarium

Your first impression as you walk into the Florida Aquarium is how huge this attraction. Signs and elevators lead off in various directions promising plenty of things to see and do. Pick up a guide of "What's swimming your way today" so you don't miss the excellent presentations that take place throughout the day at various aquarium locations.

You may want to linger at the Horseshoe Crab Observation Pool before heading up the elevator to begin your underwater adventure at the Coral Reef exhibit. This includes a huge aquarium with beautiful colored fish and mesmerizing rays that flap gently past or slide up the glass showing their amazing mouth and gills.

Shoals of silver fish swim by along with more vibrant colored species such as bright blue tangs, surgeon fish, neon-colored parrot fish, angel fish, hog fish, spotted porcupine fish and menacing open-mouthed green moray eels, among many others marine creatures.

This area includes a walk-through tunnel to see the fish, sharks and eels all around you. With various viewing windows, it's a great place for photos. The corals and anemones in the smaller side aquariums are almost as brightly colored and diverse as the fish themselves.

You'll emerge from the tunnel near the floor-to-ceiling panoramic viewing window where you can take a seat for a presentation or just sit and watch children getting up-close to sharks, giant barracuda, tarpon, grouper and turtles all so much bigger than they are!

This mega-huge aquarium is also large enough to have presentations with scientific dive masters actually inside the tank talking to the audience. They identify the various species and share some fun facts and ecological advice with the audience. The displays start with a short film promoting awareness of the fragility of our reefs and the dangers of pollution and waste disposal on the oceans.

Close by are more aquariums with the strange sea horses, pipefish and sea dragons which look like floating seaweed until you take a second look. The Ocean Commotion offers another great viewing widow to see jellyfish, octopus, crabs and countless tiny colored fish swimming in tight choreographed shoals.

The River Tales exhibit offers a change of pace with a stream with live wood ducks and ruffleheads bobbing above the fish in a cross-sectional exhibit above and below water. You'll see many of the fish that live in Florida rivers such as longnose gar, catfish and bluegill. Further on there's a huge gator display – the best way for kids to get up-close and see these scaly Florida natives in detail! Diving river otters attract attention from most youngsters as they flip and dive. Another Florida feature is the outdoor cypress swamp where herons, pink spoonbills, ducks and glossy ibis live on the water. There's a great viewing platform if you climb the steps to see the birds at eyelevel, perched in the trees.

A detour to the Rivers of Madagascar offers rainbow-colored shoals of Outer Reef Fish on beautiful corals along with a display of curious ring-tailed lemurs, also from Madagascar. After visiting the penguins, lobsters and Goliath grouper there's the opportunity to stroke stingrays in a shallow touch tank.

After a break in the café you can enjoy water in a different way, letting the kids play with water jets, cannons, fountains and slides around a pirate ship in the 2.2-acre Explore-a-Shore waterpark. Come prepared with towels, hats, sunscreen and swimsuits!

Additional Information

For an additional cost you can enjoy more unique experiences at the Florida Aquarium including:

- Penguins Backstage Pass – 30-minute experience interacting with penguins accompanied by a penguin biologist
- One-hour tour behind the scenes seeing how food is prepared and other backroom Aquarium activities
- Dive with sharks – the chance for those aged 15+ to dive with underwater instructors in the Coral Reef Gallery

- Swim with Fish – as above for swimmers aged 6+
- Stingray Feeding – a 30-minute tour learning all about stingrays and the chance to handfeed these velvety creatures
- Wild dolphin cruise – the opportunity to take a 75-minute cruise in Tampa Bay spotting dolphins and learning about local marine life. Bring binoculars!

Don't forget to bring towels and swimsuits if you want to make the most of the outdoor water play area which is included in your aquarium admission.

Admission
Adults $23.95 at the aquarium entrance, $21.95 online. Concessions for seniors and children aged 3-11.

Combo tickets are available for most add-on experiences.

Parking is $6 per day.

Opening Times
Open daily 9.30 a.m. to 5 p.m. Closed Thanksgiving and Christmas.

Where to Eat at the Florida Aquarium
Café Ray offers a good choice of healthy snacks and meals including salads, paninis, pizza and burgers in the self-service café. There is also a full-service bar and grill at the Caribbean Cantina which is open on weekends and during the peak winter season.

Nearby Attractions
- Lowry Park Zoo
- Glazer Children's Museum

Gillian Birch

15 More Ideas for Days Out with Grandkids

More family-friendly attractions from my first book *Days Out in Central Florida from The Villages:*

Cooter Pond Park and Boardwalk, Inverness

Ocklawaha River Airboat Safari

Blue Spring State Park

Central Florida Zoo, Sanford

Alexander Springs

From *Favorite Days Out in Central Florida from The Villages Residents*:

Homosassa Springs Wildlife State Park

EARS – Endangered Animal Rescue Sanctuary

Two Tails Ranch

Wild Bill's Airboat Tours

Forever Florida Swamp Buggy Coach Safari

Silver Springs Nature Theme Park

De Leon Springs State Park

Daytona Beach

From *Days Out Around Orlando*

Sponge Divers at Tarpon Springs

Winter Park Scenic Boat Ride

OVER TO YOU!

If you enjoyed this book of *Days Out from The Villages with Grandkids* and would like to recommend it to others, please consider **POSTING A SHORT REVIEW** on Amazon, Talk of the Villages website or on your favorite book review site.

Your honest opinion is truly appreciated by the author and helps other readers to judge the book fairly before buying it.

Thank you so much!

OTHER TITLES

Look out for more books and ebooks by Gillian Birch in this popular series:

- Days Out in Central Florida from The Villages
- Favorite Days Out in Central Florida from The Villages Residents
- Days Out Around Orlando
- Days Out Around Fort Myers
- 20 Best Florida Beaches and Coastal Cities
- 20 Best Historic Homes in Florida

COMING SOON

- Days Out Around Naples
- Days Out Around Orlando with Children
- Days Out Around Tampa and St Pete's
- 20 Best Gardens in Florida

These will all be available shortly in paperback and ebook format.

Keep up with future publications at: www.gillianbirch.com

ABOUT THE AUTHOR

Gillian Birch is a freelance travel writer and part-time Florida resident. As the wife of a Master Mariner, she has traveled extensively and lived in exotic locations all over the world, including Europe, the Far East, and the Republic of Panama. Her love of writing led her to keep detailed journals which are a valuable source of eye-witness information for her many published magazine articles and destination reviews.

Describing herself as having "endless itchy feet and an insatiable wanderlust," she continues to explore Florida and further afield, writing about her experiences with wonderful clarity and attention to detail.

Gillian has a Diploma from the British College of Journalism and is proud to be a member of the International Travel Writers' Alliance and the Gulf Coast Writers' Association.

Printed in the USA
CPSIA information can be obtained
at www.ICGtesting.com
LVHW012249230424
778276LV00031B/1100

9 781506 108322